AN IDEAS INTO ACTION GUIDEBOOK

Responses to Change

Helping People Manage Transition

IDEAS INTO ACTION GUIDEBOOKS

Aimed at managers and executives who are concerned with their own and others' development, each guidebook in this series gives specific advice on how to complete a developmental task or solve a leadership problem.

LEAD CONTRIBUTOR	Kerry A. Bunker
CONTRIBUTORS	Craig Chappelow
	Karen Dyer
	Bertrand Sereno
	Hughes Van Stichel
	Michael Wakefield
DIRECTOR OF PUBLICATIONS	Martin Wilcox
EDITOR	Peter Scisco
ASSOCIATE EDITOR	Karen Lewis
DESIGN AND LAYOUT	Joanne Ferguson
CONTRIBUTING ARTISTS	Laura J. Gibson
	Chris Wilson, 29 & Company

CCL No. 442
ISBN No. 978-1-60491-059-9

CENTER FOR CREATIVE LEADERSHIP
WWW.CCL.ORG

AN IDEAS INTO ACTION GUIDEBOOK

Responses to Change

Helping People Manage Transition

Kerry A. Bunker

Center for
Creative
Leadership®

THE IDEAS INTO ACTION GUIDEBOOK SERIES

This series of guidebooks draws on the practical knowledge that the Center for Creative Leadership (CCL®) has generated, since its inception in 1970, through its research and educational activity conducted in partnership with hundreds of thousands of managers and executives. Much of this knowledge is shared—in a way that is distinct from the typical university department, professional association, or consultancy. CCL is not simply a collection of individual experts, although the individual credentials of its staff are impressive; rather it is a community, with its members holding certain principles in common and working together to understand and generate practical responses to today's leadership and organizational challenges.

The purpose of the series is to provide managers with specific advice on how to complete a developmental task or solve a leadership challenge. In doing that, the series carries out CCL's mission to advance the understanding, practice, and development of leadership for the benefit of society worldwide. We think you will find the Ideas Into Action Guidebooks an important addition to your leadership toolkit.

Table of Contents

The ongoing state of many organizations is one of change. People who experience major change tend to exhibit one of four patterns of response: entrenched, overwhelmed, poser, or learner. As a leader, you need to understand the patterns of response that people express and to customize intervention strategies to help them make the transition. People can pass through a given response stage and move to one that is more effective—especially if you provide timely intervention and support. This guidebook will help you understand how people, including yourself, are responding to change and what you can do to help them move forward.

Change Happens

The ongoing, natural state of many contemporary organizations is one of change and transition. Whether arising from economic, political, technological, cultural, or societal sources, the pace and complexity of change contribute to intense emotions that play out in organizations (and outside them as well). Such reactions as fear, insecurity, uncertainty, frustration, resentment, anger, sadness, depression, guilt, distrust, and a sense of unfairness and betrayal can make it difficult for leaders to set direction, encourage alignment, and gain commitment from the people in their organizations.

Moreover, leaders aren't immune to such reactions. Faced with the turmoil of change, many leaders fall back on managing organizational processes. They fail to grasp or focus on the emotional aspects of change: grieving, letting go, building hope, and learning.

The reality is that different people can act differently and have different feelings about the changes they are experiencing. As a leader, you should not expect your direct reports, your peers, your boss, or stakeholders inside and outside your organization to share your feelings, but to act from their own points of view. At any given point in time, some will feel upbeat and energized, some anxious and tentative, and still others overwhelmed and numb. Some people may lack the requisite skills or experience needed to change and therefore remain entrenched in old behavior, while others may charge ahead with reckless abandon, seemingly oblivious to the changing demands. Still others will be upset and resistant in the short term, but primed to recover and to learn over the long haul. The change leader's challenge is to recognize and understand the patterns of response that people express as they learn their way through transition, and to customize intervention strategies that maximize the opportunity for individuals to bounce back from adversity and move forward in the evolving environment.

This guidebook presents a way of thinking about your response to change and about how others may respond. It's intended to give you a more precise understanding of the different kinds of individual and organizational responses to change, and what you can do as a leader to help people move successfully through periods of transition. Armed with that understanding, you can develop your effectiveness in helping others to understand, manage, and cope with the ambiguity and transition that mark so much of contemporary organizational life.

Often enough, simple principles lie behind some of the most effective and promising ideas. That pattern holds true in a discussion about leading during times of change, even if simple principles don't or can't capture the full complexity and difficulty people experience when their organizations undergo some kind of transformation. For the purpose of learning to lead more effectively in these circumstances, it's helpful to keep these two principles in mind:

- If you want to lead people to somewhere new, then you need to meet them where they are.
- Expect that some (even many) people aren't as far along as you would hope.

Assessing where people are in times of change involves observing the interaction between two important dimensions of their pattern of response at any given point in time: comfort with change (which includes an openness and readiness to undertake new learning) and capacity for change (which involves having the ability to learn that which is required).

Comfort with Change

Powerful change injects an emotional dynamic into the equation. Encountering a meaningful change event signals that something that previously had value and seemed to be working is suddenly being called into question or stopped altogether. Accepting and finding comfort with the change involves living through the emotional transition and coming to terms with aspects of the situation that are going away. An ending is required because we have to let go of the old way, and by association, elements of our old self. And as much as our heads might desire to slip quickly, painlessly, and seamlessly into the new circumstance, our hearts typically have a different agenda. It is often hard for us to be open and ready to take on the new challenge precisely because we have been successful at learning in the past. Something we have mastered in earlier experiences has reinforced strategies and patterns of behavior that are now an established part of our repertoire and, as such, difficult to second-guess.

Capacity for Change

Success in life is enhanced by the ability to learn, which in turn strengthens the capacity for change. Research studies of successful people confirm that they are more likely to draw important lessons from the challenges that they face, that there is a pattern to their learning efforts, that they tend to adopt a learning attitude, and that they work hard at being learners.

Unfortunately, knowing that ability to learn is an important core competency doesn't make it easy to put into practice. Indeed, going against the grain of established behavior generally results in a short-term drop in performance. Initial attempts to try out new behaviors are almost always less elegant and less successful than responding in the old way. People can be reluctant to take on a new change simply because they sense there is a likelihood of looking bad or feeling vulnerable in front of others.

Responses to Change

Figure 1 illustrates the interaction between comfort with change and capacity for change. This framework can help you assess where people in your organization *are*.

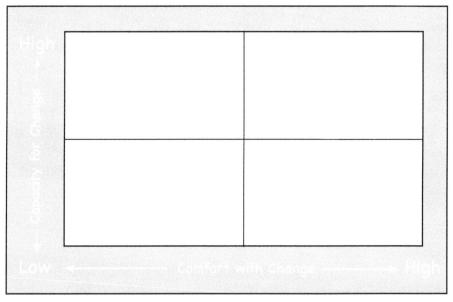

Figure 1: Patterns of response to change.

Four Responses

As you can see in figure 1, people who experience major organizational change tend to exhibit one of four patterns of response: entrenched, overwhelmed, poser, or learner. With one notable exception to be discussed later, it is important that you not label people with a given response pattern or think of their current behaviors as permanent. Indeed, people can pass through a given response stage and move to one that is more effective—especially if you provide timely intervention and support. Unfortunately, they can also revert to a less effective pattern if you fail to understand their situation or react too harshly to their transitional behavior. We'll look more closely at these leadership dynamics as we delve more deeply into the model. You may not be happy that a direct report, a peer, or even your boss stands in one of these groups, but that's where you must start if you want to lead people toward a more effective response to their challenging situation. Although there is some overlap in responses between people in these groups (what they feel, what actions they take, and how they learn), the constellation of responses among people within each group is quite distinct. Again, it's important for you as a leader to remind yourself that individuals move in and out of these groups, depending on such factors as their comfort with specific issues, the timing of events, experiences, and training. Figure 2 describes the initial reactions to change you're likely to observe among people in these four groups.

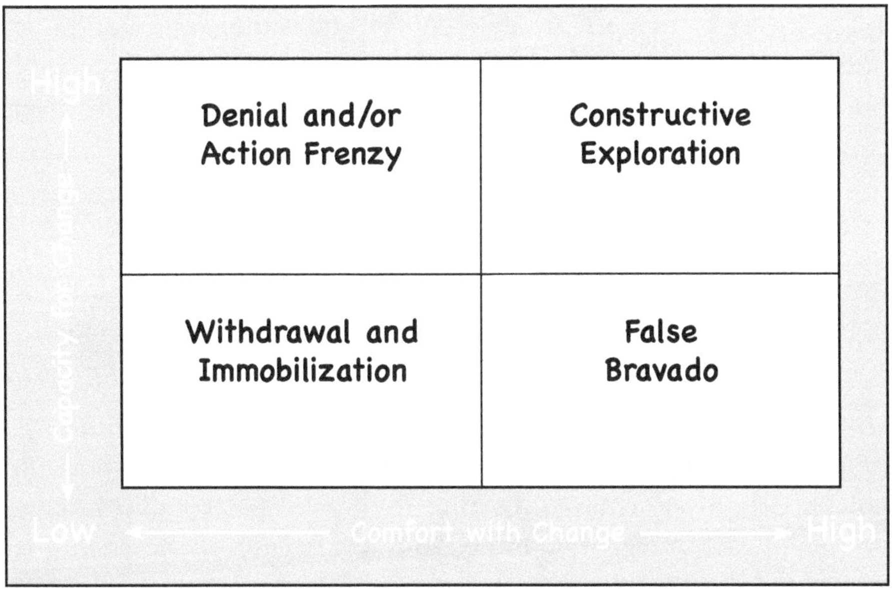

Figure 2: Initial reactions to change.

You can use the four response groups represented in figure 2 to predict such things as what behaviors to expect from people, how they will address problems, what the scope of their typical solutions will be, and how they will act as managers and leaders. As you might expect, there are other factors that influence behavior during periods of significant change and uncertainty, and there are subtle patterns of behavioral response that are not fully captured by this illustration. However, the groupings do illuminate something essential, and leaders have found this arrangement useful in dealing with the forces unleashed by organizational change and transition.

Entrenched response. People operating in the entrenched mode tend to focus on riding out the change. They sense that the known and familiar might be going away, which leads them to feel anxious and angry. They blame the organization for messing up what was working and try to keep their heads down until the leaders come to their senses. Consequently, they avoid taking risks. Typically, they can maintain their energy and continue to work hard, but they are narrow learners in the sense that they primarily rely on previously successful learning strategies and practices.

Overwhelmed response. People in this group often report feeling depressed and powerless. You may see them withdrawing from what is going on around them. Because they are spending most of their energy trying not to think too much about what is happening, they have sincere difficulty learning what is needed to survive in the new environment. Their negative mind-set can become infectious and inhibit the learning of others.

Poser response. The poser response profile represents the notable exception mentioned earlier, in that this pattern of behavior is often more enduring and linked to core elements of personality and experience. True posers have often exhibited the same behaviors over long periods of time and across a wide range of situations. People in this group express a high level of confidence about handling any change they encounter, and are always eager to move on. Unfortunately, their competence and self-awareness fail to keep pace with their bravado and self-promotion. They jockey for positions of influence and recognition but do not learn well and may lead the organization in the wrong direction.

Learner response. Learners feel challenged and stretched, but in control of their destinies. They look for opportunities in ambiguous and difficult situations and bounce back in the face of adversity. They seek to fill in gaps in their own development with learning opportunities. In most organizations these individuals tend to be at the center of the action as change unfolds. If there is a risk associated with their readiness for learning and change, it is the potential for burnout. Leadership may place excessive demands on them and look to them to be all things to all people.

Making the Transition

Your awareness of these kinds of responses certainly can help you lead people during uncertain situations, but your leading effectively depends on more than awareness—it depends on action. And while the leadership task of helping people not just survive but thrive in times of change may seem daunting, your odds will improve if you enter the situation knowing that each group has a different emotional response to confronting an uncertain future (see figure 3).

For example, people in the entrenched group don't feel ready or able to make the transition, but they often have a suppressed capacity to do it much better than they realize. If you support them in working through their emotions and guide them in accepting their capacity for change, the strength of that group can help the organization make a successful transition.

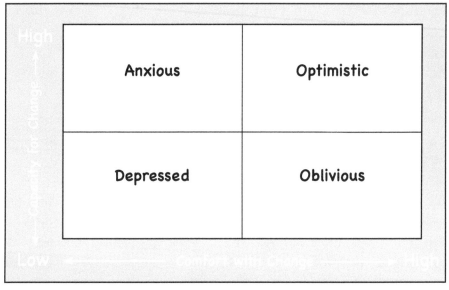

Figure 3: Feelings about an uncertain future.

People in the overwhelmed group don't feel ready or able to make the transition—and in the moment they are correct. Their ability to do it may well be limited, and their fear and withdrawal stand squarely in the way of trying. But you as the leader need to be cautious about judging too harshly or reacting too quickly. People in this response pattern often recover and learn their way to a healthier place. Getting them the training and support they need can provide a foundation for them to more fully participate in the change.

The posers in your organization probably feel more ready and able to make the transition than they really are. Their high levels of self-confidence and aggressive energy present an image that looks for all the world like the ideal employee. Unfortunately, their surface image coupled with their underlying gap in learning capacity makes true posers a significant threat to your organization. They tend to fool the leaders above them unless careful attention is focused on their actual performance and how they are perceived by others. Even then they can be difficult to develop. Your best hope is to confront their shortcomings with data and hold them accountable.

When Change Is Hardest

Perhaps the most traumatic change an organization can go through is a reorganization coupled with workforce reductions. Familiarity with the four kinds of responses can help guide your organization's leadership ranks in making the right steps toward recovery. It provides guidance on the most effective strategies for helping people who may be experiencing various elements of survivor sickness (primarily represented by expressions of the entrenched and overwhelmed responses).

For instance, although the clustering of people in each group varies from organization to organization and over time in any single organization, the mix can be particularly dysfunctional in organizations that are experiencing or recovering from downsizing. In such situations as many as 60 percent of employees may be spread across the entrenched and overwhelmed groups (percentages here and below are estimates based on work with a large number of organizations). If most of these are currently operating in the entrenched mode, then the company has its work cut out for it, but there is good reason to be optimistic. If, on the other hand, most of these are feeling and acting overwhelmed, then the situation is very difficult. Thus, a significant goal of leadership in a downsizing environment is to avoid pushing people from entrenched to overwhelmed. It's a short trip.

As for the rest, about 15 percent typically fall in the poser group, and about 25 percent are typically in the learner group. The trick here is to recognize real learners and to distinguish them from the hollow shell offered by posers. From a distance, their response patterns can look deceptively similar. Distinguishing between the two is important because the posers are not the people you want to have the most influence in difficult times.

Learners are ready and able to make the transition successfully. These people can be your allies during this period. Leadership doesn't come from just the top of the organization. If you can help learners pass their outlook and ability to learn to people in other groups, the entire organization can adapt to change more successfully.

Who Needs What?

The people in each group need distinct kinds of help to navigate the organization's transition successfully. For instance, the overwhelmed, who feel both weak and powerless, need to be developed in place rather than rushed toward empowerment in a major change of job, and they need support from superiors and peers who can, in effect, calm the waters. The entrenched, who tend to underestimate strengths and worry about weaknesses, need carefully paced learning activities (so as not to overwhelm them), a safe place to test the new things they are learning (in simulations, for instance), job opportunities that are developmental, and encouragement along with their feedback. The posers, who overestimate strengths and underestimate weaknesses, need regular, objective, and accurate feedback, and they need to focus on development rather than taking action.

How Change Can Affect Team Performance

Team leaders have different responses to change, and the leader's response can affect the team's performance.

Team actions can become . . .

narrow and fragmented when led from an *entrenched* response.	*frustrated and stuck* when led from an *overwhelmed* response.	*high performing* when led from a *learner* response.	*fearful and mistrustful* when led from a *poser* response.

The learners, who accurately assess both strengths and weaknesses, need high-impact developmental assignments, and they should be rewarded and supported for being key players in the transition process. They may also need relief from the expectation that they fill so many critical roles.

What to Look for and How to Help

There are typical feelings and behaviors for people in each group, and there are things you can do as a leader to help people in each group make the transition.

The Overwhelmed: Withdrawing and Avoiding

Faced with change, the overwhelmed may be feeling

- something between unhappiness and depression
- frustrated and anxious
- powerless and helpless
- the need for approval and reassurance
- reliant upon others
- watchful and waiting
- fearful of mistakes and failures
- a need for stability and symptom relief

Faced with change, the overwhelmed may

- block out the stressful changes
- avoid confronting issues
- retreat into safe activities
- avoid risky actions
- wait for things to return to normal
- be passive-aggressive
- seek relief of symptoms rather than solutions
- avoid thinking about what might happen

- blame and complain
- shut down, resist learning new things
- spend energy trying to look busy
- commiserate with others who feel the same way
- suggest solutions that turn back the clock
- increase or adopt unhealthy behaviors, like smoking or drinking and eating to excess

Handling Risk During Times of Change

People have different feelings about taking risks during uncertain times.

Taking risks is . . .

dangerous for the *entrenched*.	*out of the question* for the *overwhelmed*.	*an exciting opportunity* for the *learner*.	*another chance to gamble* for the *poser*.

To help the overwhelmed make a successful transition, leaders can

- make sure they can see what is actually going to change by describing what will be different going forward
- help them see what they must let go of so they can face the ending they need to make to leave the old situation behind
- recognize that they will need continuous assistance through the ending, middle, and well into the new beginning
- express understanding and provide them with personal help dealing with stress, fear, and frustration
- surround them with a manager and peers who can calm the waters around them and provide 360-degree assistance
- minimize their leadership role if they are in such positions, as they can paralyze the parts of the organization for which they are responsible
- provide a phased-in transition, with bridges to the old ways of doing things, to the degree that is possible

- have realistic expectations for their progress based on incremental movement toward accepting the new
- slow their progress toward independent actions, as cutting them loose too quickly may set them up for failure
- build changes into their current roles rather than putting them in completely new roles
- create a series of small challenges so that they can build success experiences and boost their confidence
- provide effective role models (for example, match them with someone in the learner response group)

The Entrenched: Clinging to Narrowly Defined Lessons

Faced with change, the entrenched may be feeling

- angry, frustrated, and anxious
- threatened and confused by sudden change in what kinds of behavior are valued
- confident of proven skills and past performance
- afraid of being a victim
- guilty about surviving the change if others don't
- reluctant to take action that could lead to a mistake
- unhappy, but possibly unwilling to consider a start in the external job market

Faced with change, the entrenched may

- acknowledge the need for change, but resist changing their own behavior
- work harder than ever at previously successful behavior
- avoid taking action that has any risk
- try to ride it out until things return to normal
- accept the need to change but not know how
- engage in a frenzy of activity to justify their existence
- resist new assignments that may require new learning

To help the entrenched make a successful transition, leaders can

- make sure they can see what is actually going to change by describing what will be different going forward
- help them see what they must let go of so they can face the ending they need to make to leave the old situation behind
- recognize that they will need continuous assistance through the ending, middle, and well into the new beginning
- express understanding and provide them with personal help dealing with stress, fear, and frustration
- provide carefully paced learning activities to teach new behaviors
- set realistic expectations—don't expect too much change too fast
- provide effective role models (for example, match them with someone in the learner response group)
- offer safe ways to test new behaviors or practice new roles, such as role playing and simulations
- give them frequent, positive feedback on small successes
- make sure they know that they have your continuous encouragement and support

Faced with change, posers may be feeling

- comfortable with the need for change
- anxious to move on with the transition
- surprised by and generally insensitive toward the stress or concerns expressed by others
- ready to do something, anything
- confident in their own ability to function in any situation
- possibly frustrated with the uncertainty and confusion
- irritated that others are whining

Faced with change, posers may

- press for quick solutions and decisive action
- act aggressively
- promote a pragmatic attitude but lack good solutions
- present themselves as beacons in the darkness, but ultimately become transparent
- appear to fool their bosses
- act oblivious to the challenges that lie ahead
- overestimate their strengths and fail to see weaknesses
- jockey for positions of influence and stature
- express frustration over the hesitancy of others
- push and pull others into action
- lead those in the overwhelmed response group down the wrong path

To help posers make a successful transition, leaders can

- recognize that they will be comfortable leaving the old behind, seem confident in the middle zone, but need to be reined in
- provide external checks and balances to keep them on track, as they may lack self-awareness
- resist the urge to expand their role, even though they seem ready, willing, and able
- move cautiously toward new assignments, especially high-risk ones, and insist they embrace developmental learning
- help them see what others are feeling
- provide frequent, objective assessments of their skills and learning needs
- rein in their power, which can become dangerous during major transition if they have a visible leadership position
- build in strong measures of accountability with regular reviews and monitoring
- require colleagues and boss to provide feedback on performance and behavior

- protect from self-inflicted wounds by minimizing high-visibility, high-stakes situations where they can damage their credibility and usefulness as a leader

Learners: Growing and Processing

Faced with change, learners may be feeling

- challenged and stretched
- anxious about the transition but open to the possibilities
- optimistic about the future but realistic about challenges
- in control of their own destiny and responsible for creating their own future
- not afraid to make a mistake
- more cautious than usual but still willing to push forward

Faced with change, learners may

- act positive but not unrealistically optimistic
- accept ambiguity as a challenge

When Learners Become Overwhelmed

Because people in the learner group so often respond well to change, leaders can often lean on them too heavily during times of transition. Manage the resources that learners bring to the organization by keeping your eye on a few important learner keys.

Supported Learners	Overwhelmed Learners
play key roles during change	become all things to all people
monitor the impact of change on themselves	get all the key tasks
have access to and maintain support networks	try to tough it out alone
maintain boundaries	become candidates for burnout

- accept change as an opportunity
- seek the best in even the most distressing situations
- find humor in difficult situations and use it as a tool to help others
- treat life as a continuous learning experience
- be willing to expand beyond their current comfort zone to try new things
- work to fill their own knowledge gaps through personal development
- solve problems rather than place blame
- seek out a variety of experiences and learning opportunities

To help learners make a successful transition, leaders can

- encourage and support their efforts (even though they need little help to move through a transition, don't let their needs go unmet as you focus on others who need more help)
- provide them with visible assignments in the transition
- give them high-impact roles with the latitude and resources to be successful
- make sure they have full knowledge of the big picture to provide needed context for their discussions and actions
- reward them for their support of the transition
- provide flexible growth opportunities
- encourage them to model their effective behavior for others
- let them lead and teach others throughout the transition
- assure them that moving forward, even with some mistakes, is preferable to inertia
- provide them with relief from trying to fill in too many gaps in the organization's resources

People can pass through a given response stage and move to one that is more effective—especially if you provide timely intervention and support.

How a leader's actions are seen by others is affected by the kind of response the leader has toward change.

Leadership and management styles can look like . . .

control when arising from an *entrenched* response.	*dependency* when arising from an *overwhelmed* response.	*mutual trust* when arising from a *learner* response.	*manipulation* when arising from a *poser* response.

The worksheets that follow will help you assess how people in your organization are responding to change and what you can do to help them through the period of transition.

Think of someone you work with who is having difficulty making a transition to a changed environment. The person you select might be a direct report, a peer, or even your boss. Once you have selected a person, review the material on pages 17–23 and reflect on how the person is presently behaving. You may find it helpful to place checks beside the behaviors the person is exhibiting. Then make a copy of the Response Grid Worksheet on pages 26–27 and record your observations and reflections about the person's behavior under the appropriate headings. For example, if the person overestimates his or her own strengths, note that under the Poser heading. If the person has started smoking more than before, note that under the Overwhelmed heading.

Remember that the person may be exhibiting feelings and behaviors for more than one of the response patterns. Try to identify as many examples as possible and record them under the appropriate headings. Your objective is to capture the total pattern of how the person is reacting and behaving when faced with change.

After you complete the Response Grid Worksheet, use a copy of the Intervention Planning Worksheet on page 28 to think through the initial steps for helping the person you've selected move in a more positive direction. Remember that both you and the other person will be learning as you go and that your plan may have to be modified in the face of new information or changing situations.

Use the information from the Intervention Planning Worksheet to summarize your initial intervention strategy in the space below. Outline as much of the process as possible, including tone, attitude, potential training suggestions, developmental possibilities, changes in responsibilities, and planned discussions and follow-up.

_____

_____

_____

_____

_____

_____

_____

_____

Response Grid Worksheet

Entrenched

_____

_____

_____

_____

_____

_____

_____

Overwhelmed

_____

_____

_____

_____

_____

_____

_____

_____

Learner

_____

_____

_____

_____

_____

_____

_____

Poser

_____

_____

_____

_____

_____

_____

_____

Intervention Planning Worksheet

What is the overall mood and dominant behavior pattern of this person? Which section of the Response Grid Worksheet contains most of your observations?

In general terms, how does this person need to be treated at the present time? What are the implications for your behavior? How can you best approach this person?

Are there positive aspects to how the person is feeling and acting that you need to nurture and reinforce (such as working hard, attempting to learn, exhibiting a positive attitude)?

Are there negative consequences related to the transition that require understanding, support, and guidance (such as grieving, withdrawal, feeling overwhelmed, depression, physical effects)?

Are there negative disruptive feelings and behaviors that you need to confront and monitor (such as aggressive attitudes and reactions, being stuck in overwhelmed behavior, excessive blaming, blocking the transition of others)?

Going Forward

Think of the completed worksheets not as a final resolution, but as a gateway to a better connection with the person as well as the foundation for a more impactful leadership intervention. The mere fact that you have taken the time to understand how the person is feeling and acting can often relieve some of the tension and open the door to a more open and learning-focused dialogue. An important by-product of this process is that each time you do it you'll be enhancing your own capacity to feel and express genuine empathy, support, and guidance to those around you. And there is perhaps no greater asset that a leader can bring to the table during challenging times than the authentic ability to understand, inspire, and build resiliency in others. The worksheets are there for you to use as a tool going forward. Feel free to make copies and return to them as often as you like. Whenever people are having trouble making a transition—direct reports, peers, bosses, even yourself—the worksheets will provide a tool for assessing how they are responding to change and a framework for guiding them through the transition.

Finally, it is strongly recommended that you use the worksheets to reflect on your own response to the changes unfolding around you. Wearing the mantle of leadership in no way exempts you from experiencing the fallout from change and transition. In fact, the most significant roadblock to effective transitional leadership can be that those at the leading edge often feel compelled to mask their own concerns and feelings while pressing ahead with the process. Unfortunately, masking doesn't work! Genuine optimism is important—but you can't fake it. The true pathway to empathy and authentic leadership passes directly through an honest understanding of yourself. You develop genuine emotional intelligence when you acknowledge that you are human too and that change impacts everyone. There is strength and power in having the courage to be human and vulnerable. Leading others through transition is an inside-out process that begins with the insight to lead yourself.

Suggested Readings

Bridges, W. (2004). *Transitions: Making sense of life's changes* (2nd ed.). Cambridge, MA: Da Capo Press.

Bunker, K. A., & Wakefield, M. (2010). *Leading through transitions: Participant workbook.* San Francisco: Pfeiffer.

Bunker, K. A., & Wakefield, M. (2005). *Leading with authenticity in times of transition.* Greensboro, NC: Center for Creative Leadership.

Finney, M. I. (2002). *In the face of uncertainty: 25 top leaders speak out on challenge, change, and the future of American business.* New York: AMACOM.

Klann, G. (2003). *Crisis leadership: Using military lessons, organizational experiences, and the power of influence to lessen the impact of chaos on the people you lead.* Greensboro, NC: Center for Creative Leadership.

Noer, D. M. (1995). *Healing the wounds: Overcoming the trauma of layoffs and revitalizing downsized organizations.* San Francisco: Jossey-Bass.

Sayles, L. R. (1995). *Leadership for turbulent times.* Greensboro, NC: Center for Creative Leadership.

Background

CCL's work with organizations experiencing major transitions goes back more than a dozen years, and it remains a vital and vibrant subject. The changes buffeting contemporary organizations have not ceased, and our work has grown to encompass how leaders and people at all levels of organizations respond to change, what that means in terms of handling the emotional and structural sides of transition, how organizational and leadership cultures affect change efforts, what it means to develop and coach leaders and managers so that organizations build change capability, and how people can work together across boundaries given the global scope of change and an era of uncertainty.

Today's organizations rank managing change and developing talent among the keys to competitive advantage. CCL blends change leadership and talent development into a seamless process that links to organizational strategy. CCL's practice, in areas such as organizational leadership, and its continued research, such as investigations into how interdependent leadership practices are changing the nature of leadership and organizations, continue to hold our attention and direct our efforts toward the development and practice of leadership for all times, including the most turbulent ones.

Key Point Summary

The ongoing state of many organizations is one of change. As a leader, you need to understand the patterns of response that people express and to customize intervention strategies to help them move forward.

People who experience major change tend to exhibit one of four patterns of response. Those in the entrenched group don't feel ready or able to make the transition, but they often have the capacity to do it better than they realize. Those in the overwhelmed group don't feel ready or able to make the transition—and in the moment they are correct. The posers probably feel more ready and able to make the transition than they really are. Learners are ready and able to make the transition successfully.

The people in each group need distinct kinds of help. The overwhelmed, who feel both weak and powerless, need to be developed in place, and they need support from superiors and peers. The entrenched, who tend to underestimate strengths and worry about weaknesses, need carefully paced learning activities, a safe place to test the new things they are learning, job opportunities that are developmental, and encouragement along with their feedback. The posers, who overestimate strengths and underestimate weaknesses, need regular, objective, and accurate feedback, and they need to focus on development rather than taking action. The learners, who accurately assess both strengths and weaknesses, need high-impact developmental assignments.

The included worksheets will help you assess how people are responding to change and what you can do to help them. You can also use the worksheets to reflect on your own response to the changes unfolding around you. Being a leader in no way exempts you from experiencing the fallout from change. Leading others through transition is an inside-out process that begins with the insight to lead yourself.

TO GET MORE INFORMATION, TO ORDER OTHER IDEAS INTO ACTION GUIDEBOOKS, OR TO FIND OUT ABOUT BULK-ORDER DISCOUNTS, PLEASE CONTACT US BY PHONE AT 336-545-2810 OR VISIT OUR ONLINE BOOK-STORE AT WWW.CCL.ORG/GUIDEBOOKS.

CPSIA information can be obtained
at www.ICGtesting.com
Printed in the USA
JSHW010612290421
14086JS00007B/37